Successful Dating At Last!

Another title by Jeanne "Bean" Murdock

The Every Excuse in the Book Book:
How to Benefit from Exercising, by Overcoming Your Excuses

Copyright © 2009
BeanFit Publishing
Jeanne "Bean" Murdock
Paso Robles, CA
All rights reserved

Editing, graphic design and Colophon
by Benjamin Lawless, Penciled In Designs
Printed in the United States of America by CreateSpace

Library of Congress Control Number: 2009907612
SAN: 256-6885
10-digit ISBN: 0977067815
13-digit ISBN: 9780977067817

Successful Dating At Last!
A Workbook for Understanding Each Other

By

Jeanne "Bean" Murdock, owner
BeanFit

I dedicate this book to all of the single men and women who are looking for love without having to play games. Maintain the courage to communicate effectively.

Acknowledgements

A special thanks to Sharon who inspired me to write this book and who gave me much insight on the challenges of dating. She and her boyfriend were the first to put this guide to the test—successfully!

I obtain continued appreciation for my friend, Jenny, who urges me to keep writing.

Thank you Anne & Jenny for helping me figure out this book's title.

Thank you Alouise who, by having so many bad relationships, provided me the opportunity to learn how to find the right guy the right way.

Table of Contents

Introduction, page 1

For Just You
Chapter 1. What I value in myself, page 2

Chapter 2. What I value in others, page 5

Chapter 3. My dating resume, page 8

For Both Of You

Chapter 4. What we value in each other, page 12
    Ch. 4 ½. He asks, she answers, page 15

Chapter 5. Get to know me, page 17
    Ch. 5 ½. Get to know me, too, page 25

Chapter 6. Special occasions, page 32
    Ch. 6 ½. How he feels about special occasions, page 35

Chapter 7. Ground rules, page 37
    Ch. 7 ½. What are his ground rules? page 40

Chapter 8. Sex, page 42
    Ch. 8 ½. His thoughts about sex, page 45

Chapter 9. The future, page 47
    Ch. 9 ½. His plans for the future, page 49

Conclusion, page 50

Other reading, page 51

About the author, page 52

The ½ chapters are intended for your significant other. Either let him fill it out, or ask him the questions so that you can both discuss these topics openly.

Introduction

I came up with the idea for this book when thinking about how ineffectively men and women communicate with one another and the obvious fact that they speak different languages. Listening to a girl talk about a guy she is dating, I hear that it is much more of a guessing game than it should be. You don't know if he minds being called at work? Just ask. You are afraid to ask him something because it might hurt his feelings? First of all, guys are generally less sensitive than girls. Secondly, most of the time when people are afraid that they will hurt someone's feelings, they are actually protecting their own feelings.

I have also noticed that women like men to guess what the women like, and guys just want to be told. So, I thought that if a woman came with an owner's manual, it would make forming a lasting, healthy relationship so much easier. This would be one owner's manual that a guy wouldn't throw aside and then think, "I don't need it. I can figure it out."

Use this book as a workbook to learn about yourself first. Knowing yourself will make it easier to form a healthy relationship; it also makes going through life less challenging. Second, use this book to facilitate discussion with a guy you like. It is meant for you to work in order of the chapters, but you can skip around as needed.

Another important tool in you and your boyfriend learning about each other is listening. Make sure that he stays quiet until you are done sharing. Make sure that you offer the same courtesy. Avoid saying, "You're not listening." Rather, "I need you to listen."

By the way, this workbook won't help salvage a relationship that you know is already doomed. Staying in a hopeless relationship will impair you from finding the right guy for your "owner's manual." And don't worry about having to buy another workbook each time you start a new relationship. The cost of a book is pretty small compared to the cost of staying in a bad relationship.

Enjoy filling out this workbook. Have fun learning about your boyfriend and more importantly yourself.

1
What I Value In Myself

"If she knew what she wants, he'd be giving it to her."

Lyric from "If She Knew What She Wants"
By the Bangels

Before you can find the best person for you, you need to know who you are. I used to have a client who was a child development instructor. She held workshops for teachers. With each group she asked the participants to take a few minutes to write a list of characteristics that they knew about themselves. During this time, she noticed that most of the students looked around the room blankly and did not jot any notes. How could they not know about themselves? Knowing that most of the students would write little or nothing was the purpose of including the lesson in the workshop. How could the teachers help their kids to learn about themselves if the teachers could not do the same?

When my client was done telling me the story, she asked me what I would have written. I replied, "Oh, I know a lot about myself and I find myself fascinating." That comment elicited a huge belly laugh. I do know myself well and I do find myself interesting. Peculiar, but interesting.

1994 was the year that I made a point to figure out myself and to change some of the things that I didn't like. At the end of the process, I met my soul mate who is still the love of my life. I don't think that the timing was a coincidence. Part of the process of changing me included learning how to communicate well. I know for sure that our relationship would have ended after three months, as my others did, if I had not learned how to communicate effectively.

So now it is time to learn about you as the first step in forming a lasting, healthy relationship.

When you are writing about yourself, keep in mind that it is not conceited if you write positive things about yourself.

I like this physical attribute about myself:

I like this about my personality:

Other characteristics that make me a good catch:

I ☐ ☐ believe in soul mates. Who is/was my soul mate?
   do do not

I ☐ ☐ believe in love at first sight.
   do do not

I ☐ ☐ believe in fate.
   do do not

I ☐ ☐ believe that I control most of what happens in my life.
   do do not

☐ ☐ I have no problem with commitment.
True False

I tend to choose the following type of guy:

This ☐ ☐ good.
    is isn't

Things that I would like to change about myself:

My professional goals:

My personal goals:

Where I see myself in 5 years:

Where I see myself in 10 years:

☐ ☐ I am generally a patient person.
True False

How I feel about the number of sexual partners I have had:

Are you fascinating, too? I bet you are.
This chapter opened the door for you to learn about yourself, which can be a lifelong journey.

2
What I Value In Others

It is fine to create an image in your head of the ideal guy for you. From there, you can determine your level of flexibility.

It is fine if you are set on dating your ideal guy, just as long as you don't complain about being single in the meantime.

Section 1: Ideal Looks

Hair color:

Hair (circle preferences): straight, curly, bald, long, short, doesn't matter

Eye color:

Glasses (circle preference): wears, doesn't wear

Height:

Weight:

Build/Stature:

Complexion:

Section 2: Ideal Personality

Below, write qualities that you like, e.g., funny, smart, social, quiet, life of the party, intellectual

Section 3: What You Would Like His Lifestyle To Include?

Animals:

Kids:

Married before:

Occupation:

Education level:

Ethnicity:

Languages spoken:

Religion:

Own a home:

Own a business:

Smoke:

Drink alcohol:

Type of music:

Athletic:

Cultural/Artistic:

Income:

Mechanically inclined:

Musically inclined:

In the next chapter, fill in your dating history and reason for dating—your dating objective. Afterward, read what you wrote and see if it matches what you entered in this chapter. Did you date guys who matched your ideal image, were they complete opposites, or somewhere in between?

You don't have to make excuses for a failed relationship, but hopefully chapter 3 will help you to learn why each ended. Critiquing excuses should be reserved for your reasons for staying in a failing relationship.

3

My Dating Resume

Sample

Dating Objective

To find a guy to marry and to share the rest of my life.

Education: What I Learned About Past Relationships

John: We had a lot of fun together. He was married and promised to leave his wife. After 4 years, he still hadn't left his wife. Conclusion: he was just stringing me along.

Chris: We had a committed relationship. He asked me to marry him and to move to Australia with him. He was a British citizen who moved around a lot. Conclusion: he wanted to become an American citizen.

Steve: We had a committed relationship, but he teased me a lot. Also, he did not support me professionally. Conclusion: he was insecure.

Experience: Past Relationships

John: 2002-2006, I loved him.

Chris: 1995-2000, I loved him, first love.

Steve: 1994-1995, I did not love him.

A blur: prior to 1994

Other Interests

Occasional one-night stands.

Dating Objective

Education: What I Learned About Past Relationships

❶ Name:

Summary:

Conclusion:

❷ Name:

Summary:

Conclusion:

❸ Name:

Summary:

Conclusion:

❹ Name:

Summary:

Conclusion:

Use a separate sheet of paper to extend the list.

Experience: Past Relationships

❶ Name

Year(s) dated:

I ☐ ☐ him.
  loved didn't love

❷ Name

Year(s) dated:

I ☐ ☐ him.
  loved didn't love

❸ Name

Year(s) dated:

I ☐ ☐ him.
  loved didn't love

❹ Name

Year(s) dated:

I ☐ ☐ him.
  loved didn't love

❺ Name

Year(s) dated:

I ☐ ☐ him.
  loved didn't love

❻ Name

Year(s) dated:

I ☐ ☐ him.
  loved didn't love

❼ Name

Year(s) dated:

I ☐ ☐ him.
  loved didn't love

Use a separate sheet of paper to extend the list.

Other Interests:

4

What We Value In Each Other

This chapter is designed to facilitate conversation regarding what you and your new guy like about each other.

You can ask a question like, "What did you first notice about me?" and then fill in his response. Chapter 4½ provides the opportunity for him to ask you the same questions.

What did you first notice about me?

Were you nervous to talk to me the first time?

What do you think about my friends whom you've met, so far?

What do you think about my family, so far?

What do you think is my most valuable feature?

What are some traits that you value in me?

What characteristics do you think make us compatible?

What makes it easy for us to get along?

What do you like about us as a couple?

Chapter 4½: He asks, she answers

What did you first notice about me?

Were you nervous to talk to me the first time?

What do you think about my friends whom you've met, so far?

What do you think about my family, so far?

What do you think is my most valuable feature?

What are some traits that you value in me?

What characteristics do you think make us compatible?

What makes it easy for us to get along?

What do you like about us as a couple?

5

Get To Know Me

This chapter is designed for you to fill out on your own. When you're ready and comfortable enough to open up to the guy you're dating, you can go through this chapter together.

Then, he can fill in his own responses in chapter 5 ½, so that you can get to know him, too.

My best friend is:

My birthday:

I ☐ ☐ have friends of the opposite sex.
   do do not

This is how I feel about keeping my guy friends and how I feel about jealousy:

These are feelings that are difficult for me to express:

When I don't feel well, I would like it if you would:

When I get angry I need you to:

This is what I am like when I'm stressed:

I have the following food/chemical sensitivities:

My ideal vacation:

How many children I have and would like to have:

Previous marriages:

How I feel about getting married (again?):

How I feel about developing a new, serious relationship:

I'll tell you about siblings:

I'll tell you about my parents:

My culture/ethnicity/religion:

How I feel about going to church:

How I feel about reading the bible:

Interesting story about when I was born:

I tend to be ☐ ☐ ☐ .
           neat messy in between

My hobbies:

I ☐ ☐ dancing.
  like don't like

Sports I like to play:

Sports I like to watch:

My favorite teams:

Cultural events I like (e.g., opera, ballet, museum):

I would rather ☐ ☐ .
              cook eat out

My Favorites:

Movie:

Actor:

Comedian:

Flower:

Holiday:

Perfume/Cologne:

Musical instrument:

Gemstone:

My birthstone:

Color:

Song:

Type of music:

Band/Singer:

Other topics:

My best life experience, so far:

My pet peeves:

My superstitions:

How much traveling I have done and how much I would still like to do:

How I feel about illegal drugs:

How I feel about alcohol:

How I feel about surprises:

How I feel about practical jokes:

My fears/phobias:

Disease(s) and condition(s) that I have:

Criminal record:

My ideal date:

☐ ☐ I like it when doors are opened for me.
True False

☐ ☐ I like it when things are done for me.
True False

How I feel about my independence:

The types of gifts I like to receive:

What I consider romantic:

How I define love:

Chapter 5 ½: Get to know me, too.

My best friend is:

My birthday:

I ☐ ☐ have friends of the opposite sex.
  do do not

This is how I feel about keeping my friends of the opposite sex and how I feel about jealousy:

These are feelings that are difficult for me to express:

When I don't feel well, I would like it if you would:

When I get angry I need you to:

This is what I am like when I'm stressed:

I have the following food/chemical sensitivities:

My ideal vacation:

How many children I have and would like to have:

Previous marriages:

How I feel about getting married (again?):

How I feel about developing a new, serious relationship:

I'll tell you about siblings:

I'll tell you about my parents:

My culture/ethnicity/religion:

How I feel about going to church:

How I feel about reading the bible:

Interesting story about when I was born:

I tend to be ☐ ☐ ☐ .
              neat messy in between

My hobbies:

I ☐ ☐ dancing.
 like don't like

Sports I like to play:

Sports I like to watch:

My favorite teams:

Cultural events I like (e.g., opera, ballet, museum):

I would rather ☐ ☐ .
             cook eat out

My Favorites:

Movie:

Actor:

Comedian:

Flower:

Holiday:

Perfume/Cologne:

Musical instrument:

Gemstone:

My birthstone:

Color:

Song:

Type of music:

Band/Singer:

Other topics:

My best life experience, so far:

My pet peeves:

My superstitions:

How much traveling I have done and how much I would still like to do:

How I feel about illegal drugs:

How I feel about alcohol:

How I feel about surprises:

How I feel about practical jokes:

My fears/phobias:

Disease(s) and condition(s) that I have:

Criminal record:

My ideal date:

☐ ☐ I like it when things are done for me.
True False

How I feel about my independence:

The types of gifts I like to receive:

What I consider romantic:

How I define love:

6
Special Occasions

Aww. Special occasions. From birthdays to holidays. Do you hate them? Love them? Communicate how you feel about each occasion, how you would like to observe it if at all, and what type of gift exchanging you like if at all. This list could include regular family gatherings at certain times of the year.

Move onto chapter 6 ½ when your boyfriend is ready to share his own desires for special occasions.

Valentine's Day:

St. Patrick's Day:

Easter:

Memorial Weekend:

Fourth of July:

Labor Day:

Halloween:

Thanksgiving:

Christmas:

New Year's Eve:

My birthday:

Anniversary of:

Chapter 6 ½: How He Feels About Special Occasions

Valentine's Day:

St. Patrick's Day:

Easter:

Memorial Weekend:

Fourth of July:

Labor Day:

Halloween:

Thanksgiving:

Christmas:

New Year's Eve:

My birthday:

Anniversary of:

7
Ground Rules

This chapter is called "Ground Rules," otherwise known as boundaries. One way to think about boundaries is that they are like a code of ethics—actions that you allow according to what makes you comfortable.

Discuss behaviors you like and dislike up front, so that you avoid assumptions. Make time for your boyfriend to explain his boundaries by utilizing chapter 7 ½.

This is how I feel about us publicly displaying affection:

I ☐ ☐ consider myself a touchy person.
   do do not

I ☐ ☐ consider myself a jealous person.
   do do not

How I feel about committing to you at this point:

How I feel about dating others, kissing others, sex with others (swinging):

For now, let's not talk about:

If you cheat, this is what you should expect from me:

If I cheat, I would expect you to:

I feel uncomfortable when you:

In our relationship, I would like from you:

Chapter 7 ½: What Are His Ground Rules?

This is how I feel about us publicly displaying affection:

I ☐ ☐ consider myself a touchy person.
  do do not

I ☐ ☐ consider myself a jealous person.
  do do not

How I feel about committing to you at this point:

How I feel about dating others, kissing others, sex with others (swinging):

For now, let's not talk about:

If you cheat, this is what you should expect from me:

If I cheat, I would expect you to:

I feel uncomfortable when you:

In our relationship, I would like from you:

8
Sex

If you can't talk with your boyfriend about sex, then you shouldn't be intimate with him. Sex is a serious topic and should be discussed honestly and openly first. Remember, sex makes babies. It also can lead to sexually transmitted diseases (STD) that kill.
Did you know that the human papilloma virus (HPV), which causes genital warts, can lead to cervical cancer?

Would you have sex with a man who has an STD? How would you know he has one if you don't ask? Do you trust him enough to believe his answer? How does he know for sure that he doesn't have one if he has not been screened?

Some pathogens do not cause signs or symptoms in the carrier and therefore require more detective work to diagnose, yet can still be transmitted. Some tests require blood work and others involve swabbing the genital areas. Consider visiting a clinic together to be screened for STD's before having sex for the first time.

This chapter is a means to get you started in talking about sex with your boyfriend. You can ask him these questions and then move onto chapter 8 ½ to give him the chance to query you.

Do you like French kissing?

How long do you want to wait before we have sex?

How many sexual partners have you had?

Are you willing to have STD testing?

Have you ever had an STD?

Have you ever been tested for an STD?

How old were you when you first had sex?

How do you like to be touched sexually?

What type of sex toys, if any, do you like to use?

How do you see pornographic movies fitting into our relationship?

How do you feel about us being filmed?

How do you feel about abortion? What if it's our baby?

To learn more about your body, sex, and sexually transmitted diseases I recommend:

Websites
    www.plannedparenthood.org
    www.aids.org
    www.cdc.gov/std

Book
    Boston Women's Health Book Collective, Norsigian, J. *Our Bodies, Ourselves*. Touchstone. 2005.

Chapter 8 ½: His Thoughts About Sex

Do you like French kissing?

How long do you want to wait before we have sex?

How many sexual partners have you had?

Are you willing to have STD testing?

Have you ever had an STD?

Have you ever been tested for an STD?

How old were you when you first had sex?

How do you like to be touched sexually?

What type of sex toys, if any, do you like to use?

How do you see pornographic movies fitting into our relationship?

How do you feel about us being filmed?

How do you feel about abortion? What if it's our baby?

9
The Future

If you would like to have a long-term relationship, you need to make sure that your boyfriend's long-term goals complement yours. You don't need to wait until you have been dating a couple of years to determine if your prospective futures match. In fact, you don't even have to go through the first eight chapters of this book first.

I know a girl who, upon meeting a nice guy, asks him her standard ten questions. That way she could quickly sift through the incompatible guys without going through the pain of dating and breaking up.

Use the list below to share what you hope for your future and then move onto chapter 9 ½ to allow your boyfriend to share his perspective.

How many kids I would like to have:

What type of home I would like to have:

Where I would like to live next:

When I would like to retire and what I imagine retirement to be like for myself:

Current living situation with existing (if any) kids and how that may change in the future:

Things I can't accept about you. Things that would prevent me from moving forward with you:

In order to move forward with our relationship I am willing to change:

Chapter 9 ½: His Plans for the Future

How many kids I would like to have:

What type of home I would like to have:

Where I would like to live next:

When I would like to retire and what I imagine retirement to be like for myself:

Current living situation with existing (if any) kids and how that may change in the future:

Things I can't accept about you. Things that would prevent me from moving forward with you:

In order to move forward with our relationship I am willing to change:

Conclusion

Dating and learning about someone new should be fun and exciting. Hopefully, this manual helped you to understand yourself and taught you how to communicate effectively with your boyfriend.

Even dating someone compatible with you may bring challenges, but if you two are meant to be together your life will be enriched.

Other Reading

Behrendt, G, Tuccillo, L. *He's Just not that into You: The no-Excuses Truth to Understanding Guys.* Element. 2005.

Murdock, J. *The Every Excuse in the Book Book: How to Benefit from Exercising, by Overcoming Your Excuses.* BeanFit Publishing. 2005.

Simon, S, Howe, L, Kirschenbaum, H. *Values Clarification.* Warner Books. 1995.

Tannen, D. *You Just Don't Understand.* Ballantine Books. 1991.

About The Author

Jeanne "Bean" Murdock brings a new approach to health and fitness consulting, fusing time management and life organization techniques with exercise tips to devise innovative strategies for people to fit a comprehensive exercise, nutrition and healthy living program into their lives, no matter how hectic. She also consults businesses on efficiency and how to accommodate the changing health needs of their customers.

Through her counseling and lectures, her books and articles, her many radio appearances, and now her new TV show, Jeanne uses a combination of knowledge and humor to educate the public on a wide variety of health and fitness topics and to change lives. Her compassionate approach inspires people from every background and health status.

Originally from Cupertino, CA, Jeanne studied physical education at California Polytechnic State University in San Luis Obispo, and then started BeanFit Health and Fitness Services in 1992. Since February 2004, she has been living in Paso Robles, CA, and continuing to serve clients throughout North America.

- Bachelor of Science in Physical Education, concentration in Commercial/Corporate Fitness, Cal Poly State University, San Luis Obispo.
- Undergraduate Nutrition Coursework Completed, San Diego State University.
- Chairman, SLO County Celiacs San Luis Obispo County.

Memberships:
- Gluten Intolerance Group
- American College of Sports Medicine
- Food Allergy and Anaphylaxis Network

Photo of Jeanne "Bean" Murdock by Kurt O. Brown

*Visit www.beanfit.com for the story
behind the cover photo.*

"Treat Yourself to a Healthy Lifestyle"

BeanFit®

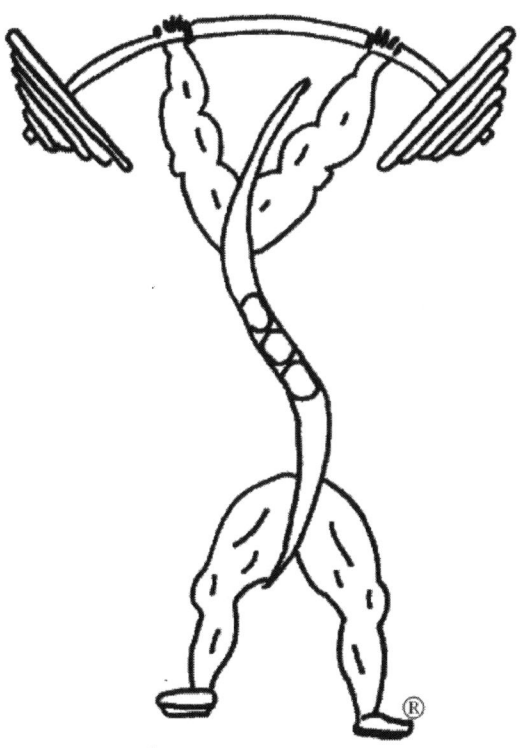

Health and Fitness Services

Questions? Comments?
Please feel free to write or call Jeanne "Bean" Murdock anytime at:

BeanFit
P. O. Box 1083
Paso Robles, CA 93447
Phone/Fax: 805-226-9893
Website: www.beanfit.com
E-mail: info@beanfit.com

Visit www.beanfit.com to sign up for
a free monthly e-newsletter.

Colophon

The main text of this book is set in the stately Hoefler Text, designed by Jonathan Hoefler of Hoefler & Frere Jones for Apple Computer in 1991. It was one of the first examples of fine typographical prowess in a digital typeface. Even though it has been bundled with every version of the Macintosh operating system since System 7.5, this designer would like to point out that it is a perfectly well-suited font for the work in which it is employed, and that he is still the epitome of a font snob, thank you very much.

In stark contrast, the chapter titles have been set in the playful Fontana ND, designed by Rubén Fontana in 2001. The font was built to showcase a unique visual identity that draws upon Spanish and Native American roots. This designer was sold on the capital Q in the font (see the previous page).

The cover and bastard title page were set in Helvetica, of which much has been written. The symbols for the numbers 0-9 in chapter 3 is none other than good ol' Wingdings. Yes, the designer went there, but it worked!

The book itself was laid out in Adobe InDesign CS4 on a brand spanking new MacBook Pro 2.53 GHz Intel Core 2 Duo running Snow Leopard. And yes, this hipster designer also has a fauxhawk. Try not to faint.

Made in the USA